GREAT WESTERN
PICTORIAL

GREAT WESTERN
PICTORIAL

PHILIP HOPKINS

ISBN 1 874103 22 4

Designed by Paul Karau
Printed by Amadeus Press Ltd, Huddersfield

Published by
WILD SWAN PUBLICATIONS LTD.
1-3 Hagbourne Road, Didcot, Oxon, OX11 8DP

Having completed the stiff climb up the 1 in 42 of Hemerdon bank, 'Bulldog' 4-4-0 No. 3445 *Goldfinch* and Old Oak 'County' class 4-6-0 No. 1015 *County of Dorset* are pictured on the less demanding section leading to the summit at Wrangaton with a Newquay to Paddington service, c.1947. The train had just passed through Cornwood, whose down distant signal can be seen on the left. The assisting 'Bulldog' was allocated to Laira, one of six at the shed at that time, whilst Newton Abbot had five; between them, they handled many of the banking duties over the inclines of South Devon.

CONTENTS

'Bulldog' 4-4-0 No. 3409 *Queensland* alongside the up main platform at Worcester Shrub Hill in the mid-1930s with a goods train from the Hereford line. This engine was built in 1904 as No.3471, and was sent to her first shed, Neath, in June of that year. *Queensland* remained at various sheds in West Wales until 1917, having been renumbered to 3409 in December 1912. She was transferred to Wolverhampton during 1917, and on to the Worcester division in 1922, where she resided at Gloucester and Hereford sheds until her withdrawal in January 1939.

INTRODUCTION

My early interest in railways was stimulated by watching express trains speeding along the Great Western Railway main line between Birmingham (Snow Hill) and London (Paddington). Soon after the age of double figures, I became the proud owner of a 'Box Brownie' and started taking photographs of trains, nearly seventy years ago. This camera was replaced in due course with a better one which had a shutter speed of 1/200th second, and took postcard-sized negatives.

Although this collection is mainly Great Western pictures, I was only able to cover a very small part of the railway due to the limited amount of pocket money which I was allowed as a young boy. Fortunately, my parents enjoyed the odd trip to the Cotswolds, and a holiday or two in the West Country which gave me the opportunity to photograph other parts of the Great Western.

I would like to thank John Copsey for his great help in preparation of the captions and I hope that the photographs included in this book will be of interest to the reader, who will doubtless share with me the love of things Great Western.

P. A. HOPKINS
West Midlands
1995

One of the most versatile designs to emerge from Swindon was the '2301' class 0-6-0, of which 260 examples (excluding the twenty '2361' variants) were built between 1883 and 1899. Although they were nominally goods engines, the class was regularly used on local passenger trains on many parts of the system, from their early days. For example, during the summer of 1894 they were recorded on Swansea to Carmarthen, Oxford to Paddington, Taunton to Liskeard, Hereford to Gloucester and Paddington to Frome services, plus a number of turns on secondary expresses to South Wales and the West Country, at a time when 2-4-0s and 4-2-2s reigned supreme. In this view, Worcester's No. 2557 is seen on a rather more mundane duty, a 'K' class pick-up goods, during the 1930s. She was at Worcester between 1932 and 1939, working alongside a number of sister engines on such turns as the 5.50 a.m. local goods to Highley, the 10.15 passenger (Saturdays) onwards to Bridgnorth, 10.41 light engine to Highley, and the 11.50 local goods thence back to Worcester; Saturdays excepted, she returned from Highley with the 10.50 local goods. The engines were also recorded on such local goods turns as the 4.35 a.m. to Moreton-in-Marsh, 9.50 a.m. to Bromyard, 10.30 a.m. to Leominster, and the 3.40 p.m. to Kidderminster, amongst others. No. 2557 was withdrawn in 1940 for Government service.

Between 1926 and 1936, 'Bulldog' No. 3341 *Blasius* was stationed at Reading, sharing mostly passenger turns with a number of sister engines there. In 1928 these duties took the engines on daily runs to Paddington, Oxford, Bristol, Westbury, Portsmouth and Southampton. *Blasius* is pictured on the middle relief road at Reading around 1932, possibly awaiting an up semi-fast to take on to Paddington. She survived until November 1949, a working life of almost fifty years.

READING

An empty stock train on the down main passing Reading Main Line East box in the mid-1930s behind 'Castle' class 4-6-0 No. 111 *Viscount Churchill*, an engine which spent the whole of its Great Western career at Old Oak shed. She carries the pre-1936 headlamp code 'D'; in that year, the arrangement of lamps for 'D' was changed, so the centre lamp was positioned over the buffer beam instead of in front of the chimney, whilst the other remained over the left-hand buffer (as viewed from the front). This alteration separated it visually from class 'C' trains, with which the lamp code had originally been shared, although the empty coaching stock trains always had their own distinctive bell code for signalling purposes.

'Bulldog' No. 3394 *Albany* waiting in the up relief bay (No. 6 Bay) platform c.1930. The engine was fitted with the Westinghouse brake system, which enabled it to operate such fitted stock from the Great Eastern, and London, Brighton & South Coast railways, often as special trains. Along with six other Westinghouse engines (four 'Bulldogs', an 'Atbara', and latterly a '63XX'), *Albany* was allocated to Old Oak or Reading, though she spent the last couple of years of her life at Worcester (by which time the Westinghouse equipment had probably been removed). These locomotives operated normal services when not required for the specials; Old Oak, for example, used its Westinghouse 'Bulldogs' mostly on West London line work.

In September 1934, the new '48XX' class 0-4-2 tank No. 4838 was transferred from Swindon works to Reading shed to join her sister engine No. 4827, which had arrived there during the previous November. These replaced two '517' class engines which had been employed on auto services from Reading, although other engines of that elderly class were still to be found periodically at the shed, along with the odd 'Metro'. The '48s' were rostered to run two 2-car auto sets between Reading, Goring, Basingstoke, Henley-on-Thames, Maidenhead, Bourne End and Marlow during the mid-1930s. No. 4838 is pictured taking water at the up relief platform at Reading c.1935, attached to 'Clifton Down' stock.

At approximately 4.29 p.m. each weekday, the 'Cheltenham Flyer' was due to pass through Reading station at speeds frequently between 80 and 90 m.p.h. In this view, 'Castle' 4-6-0 No. 5018 *St. Mawes Castle* was bringing the train through on the main, with a thirty-one minute schedule ahead of her to Paddington, some thirty-six miles distant; such was her speed on this occasion that she 'purred' through the station. This was an Old Oak turn in which the engine traditionally took the 10.45 a.m. Paddington to Cheltenham train as far as Gloucester, returning from that station with the 'Flyer', 2.40 p.m. from Cheltenham. Through the 'thirties, this train normally consisted of between four and six vehicles from Cheltenham, a Dining Car from Gloucester and a Brake Compo from Hereford (also attached at Gloucester). In the early 1930s the 2.40 Cheltenham was the fastest train in the world, with an average start to stop speed of 71.4 m.p.h. between Swindon and Paddington; accordingly, as seen here, the locomotive carried a headboard proclaiming this achievement in addition to the winged 'Cheltenham Flyer'. In the mid 'thirties, the 'Flyer' was ousted from her pinnacle, and a plain headboard inscribed 'Cheltenham Flyer' was used thereafter.

'2221' class 4-4-2T No. 2247 in one of the down bays at the west end of Reading station, c.1932, possibly on a Basingstoke train. With the introduction of the '61XX' class 2-6-2Ts for accelerated suburban services in 1931, the days of the County Tanks were numbered, although they were still to be seen on such trains until at least 1934. No. 2247 was allocated to Reading for a spell during 1932/33, and was withdrawn from service in November 1933.

Another '2221' class 4-4-2T, No. 2243, is seen here at the west end of Reading station on the down relief line during the early 1930s. Prior to the introduction of the '61s', the class was much favoured for the Paddington & Reading services, and Reading itself generally had four or five examples in residence. No. 2243 was probably on a passenger pilot duty on this occasion, which normally involved two or three engines for most of the day at this time. Withdrawal of the class commenced in 1931, with the last three going in 1935, all effectively from Reading; indeed, of the thirty engines, eleven ended their working lives there.

The bay at the west end of the central island platform (No. 4 West Bay) at Reading was used mostly for local departures on the Oxford or Swindon lines, though trains for the Berks & Hants route also made use of it. This picture shows 'County' class 4-4-0 No. 3807 in No. 4 West Bay during September 1929, probably with the 10.48 a.m. service to Didcot and Oxford, the return working of her scheduled 8.32 a.m. Didcot to Reading turn. This engine was completed in November 1906, and spent her first few years at Old Oak shed, though with short spells at Wolverhampton, Exeter, Bristol and Weymouth. After the outbreak of the Great War, 3807 was transferred to Cardiff, Bristol, Worcester and Wolverhampton, continuing her wanderings in 1924 to Swindon and Westbury. During the last two years of her life, she resided at Old Oak, Oxford and Didcot, working largely on local or semi-fast passenger trains, before being withdrawn from Didcot in November 1930.

Didcot's '2251' class 0-6-0 No. 2259 in No. 4 Bay at the west end of Reading with a local passenger train, probably destined for her home town, c.1935. She was allocated to Didcot in April 1930, when new, and spent the years up to 1938 mostly on goods turns, being a regular performer on the 3.52 a.m. to Oxley Sidings (up to 66 wagons) and the 7.35 a.m. Wednesbury return trip on the following day. However, she was occasionally used on passenger duties on the main and DN & S lines. Reading Middle signal box can be seen to the left of the engine.

The impressive lines of the '61XX' tanks are seen to advantage in this photograph of No. 6105, viewed at the down main platform at Reading with a milk empties train c.1932. Delivered in June 1931, No. 6105 spent her entire GWR career at Slough, working alongside her numerous sisters there, mostly on passenger services to and from Paddington, Windsor, Aylesbury, and Reading.

The most important connection between the LNER and the Great Western was at Banbury, where a large amount of traffic, both passenger and goods, was transferred. Having turned at the shed, LNE 'C4' (ex-GC) 4–4–2 No. 5261, probably from Woodford, is shown here drifting on the down main alongside Banbury's goods shed, c.1932; it was about to pass through the passenger station on its way to the north end, where it awaited the arrival of its through train, which it probably worked on to either Leicester or Sheffield. At this time, there were five daily LNER expresses in each direction, running to and from Southampton, Bournemouth or Swansea and Newcastle, and Swindon and York (including the Penzance & Aberdeen and Penzance & Glasgow through running to and from Swindon was part of the arrangement. services, though periodic through running to Swindon was part of the arrangement.

BANBURY

With a couple of exceptions, the '2221' class engines were based in the London division throughout their working lives; one such exemption was the prototype, No. 2221, which spent the years up to 1921 at Trowbridge. Although they largely worked within their home division, the '2221s' were regularly to be seen in neighbouring areas, and handled fast services daily between Paddington, Swindon and Bristol prior to the First World War. No. 2239 was a Slough engine for many years, and was sometimes utilised on the 7.22 a.m. service to Banbury; she is seen here at the down platform at Banbury, c.1931, possibly with that train.

LNER 'C4' class 4-4-2 No. 6088 departing from the down platform at Banbury with a Newcastle train in the early 1930s. The train ran northwards on the main line for about a mile before turning off at Banbury Junction onto LNE metals, with a nine-mile journey ahead of it to the ex-Great Central main line at Culworth Junction, a mile or so to the south of Woodford & Hinton. In addition to the regular expresses, the line would see a number of through specials, including many to the south coast at holiday periods; with these extra engine changes, Banbury became a very busy location at such times.

The south end of Leamington Spa station in the early 1930s, looking northwards from the down platform. Built upon the site of a large block of Georgian buildings, Eastnor Terrace, the station originally had an overall roof, the remains of which were incorporated into the roofing of the platform buildings. Shortly after its opening in 1852, Leamington became the terminal point for several trains to and from Birmingham, heralding its future role as the southern limit of the numerous suburban sets is seen at the up platform in this view. The large signal gantry on the right was supported by two separate posts, set into the platform, and had a considerable overhang across the up platform line to allow sighting by up trains.

LEAMINGTON SPA

Banbury's 'Bulldog' No. 3383 *Ilfracombe* pictured with an up local passenger train at Leamington, c.1929. The name was removed in the summer of 1930, apparently to avoid confusion with train destinations. At this time, the Banbury 'Bulldogs' were scheduled to operate two passenger and one goods turn daily, with one of the passenger duties reaching Birmingham.

The '36XX' class 2-4-2Ts were introduced in 1902, and by 1906 about two-thirds of them were resident in the Birmingham and northern areas, a figure which remained fairly constant until their demise in the early 1930s. In this view, No. 3616 is seen at the up platform at Leamington with a passenger train from Stratford in August 1931. She spent some time at Stratford between 1930 and 1933, the year of her withdrawal, and must have been a fairly regular visitor to Leamington during that period. The engines could take up to eleven bogies on the route from Leamington to Wolverhampton, and a similar figure through to Stratford.

'Castle' class 4-6-0 No. 4089 *Donnington Castle* waiting alongside the up platform at Leamington Spa, during September 1929. At that time she was one of Old Oak's 'Castles', which were often used to work the 11.45 a.m. Birkenhead from Wolverhampton to Paddington, and the 9.35 a.m. Birkenhead to Bournemouth as between Wolverhampton and Oxford. On the run to Paddington via Bicester, the 'Castle' could take 455 tons on the normal schedule, some fourteen coaches, one or two less than the 'King' class. By the latter part of 1929 many of the 'Castles' had acquired 4,000 gallon tenders, though others retained the 3,500 type up to 1931.

During the early 1930s, the '43XX' 2-6-0s were the primary class of engine on goods services over the Wolverhampton line, and could be seen hauling most types of train. They were frequently used on the vacuum services alongside the '47XXs' and '49XXs', and on the slower, heavier trains to and from London and Reading with the '28XXs', and '30XXs'. No. 6329 was built in 1921, leaving Swindon factory on 3rd May of that year. Her first shed was Old Oak, though in 1925, she was transferred to the Wolverhampton division. Initially shedded at Birkenhead, No. 6329 subsequently moved to Chester, Oxley, Stafford Road and Banbury until, in 1944, she was transferred south to Didcot; during the interwar period, therefore, she was no stranger to the Northern line. She is seen here taking water at Leamington, at the head of a 'C' class vacuum goods, c.1930.

It was not often that the ex-M&SWJ 4-4-0s strayed very far from their home territory, but No. 1125 is pictured here at Leamington Spa in September 1929 with an up vacuum goods. Stationed at Cheltenham (High Street), No. 1125 is recorded as spending a short period at Worcester in the latter part of 1929, and was most probably working a fruit special from the Vale of Evesham via Honeybourne and Stratford, possibly for the LNER at Banbury. Examples of the nine Tyrell 4-4-0s taken into GWR stock survived until 1938, though No. 1125 was condemned in February 1932.

The last of the 'Stars' appeared in early 1923, just a few months before the introduction of the 'Castles'. Amongst the final batch was No. 4070 *Neath Abbey*, which went to Stafford Road shed when new in February 1923; she is seen here at the up platform at Leamington in September 1929 with a southbound express. The fourteen 'Stars' still reigned supreme on express duties at Stafford Road, which had just two 'Kings' and two 'Castles' allocated at this time. *Neath Abbey* spent periods at Newton Abbot, Laira, Exeter, Cardiff, Landore and Gloucester in addition to her spells at Stafford Road. She was withdrawn in January 1939, and reappeared as 'Castle' class No. 5090 in May of that year, still carrying the same name.

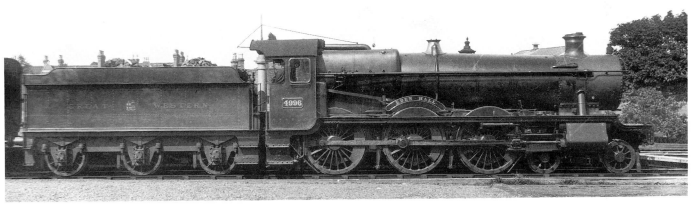

'Hall' class 4-6-0 No. 4996 *Eden Hall* at Leamington Spa with an up parcels in 1931. This engine first entered traffic in March 1931 coupled to Collett 3,500 gallon tender No. 2266, but, after a light repair at Swindon at the end of that year, she was given a new 4,000 gallon tender. Thereafter she ran with the larger capacity ones, though on two occasions she was coupled to examples of those built under Dean in 1900/01. Between 1960 and 1962, she also ran with a Hawksworth pattern tender. An Old Oak engine at this time, she would have been found on many of the routes out of London, and is recorded as having worked the 6.35 p.m. Oxford to Paddington (via Thame) on 31st July 1931, and the 4.27 p.m. milk train from Weymouth to Westbury on 29th February 1932.

The large 'Prairies' of the '31XX' class were established at Leamington before the First World War, primarily for goods duties to Banbury, Oxford, and even Old Oak Common. However, it was not until 1928/9 that the class (renumbered into the '51XX' series), followed by members of the new '5101' series, were allocated to the Birmingham area in large numbers to take over the suburban passenger duties from the '36XX' 2-4-2Ts and '39XX' 2-6-2Ts. '51XX' No. 5121 arrived at Leamington during the latter part of 1929, and is pictured here at the London end of the down platform on a local passenger duty c.1930. She survived until October 1948, with a working life spanning 43 years.

Leamington Spa station, looking towards London from the down main platform in 1929, with a Birmingham divisional four-coach suburban set on the up main, and a '43XX' and coaches (probably through vehicles from Stratford-on-Avon) waiting in the up bay for the arrival of a London-bound express, when the coaches would be attached to the rear. This procedure was carried out two or three times a day during this period, mostly with returning slip vehicles that had been detached previously at Leamington (for onward conveyance to Stratford) from down Paddington expresses. The public footbridge in the foreground was some 130 yards in length, and connected the Old Warwick Road (on the south side of the GWR station) with the north side of the LMS company's Avenue station. It crossed over the down bays (on the right), the four main running roads, the up bay, two goods running loops (to the left of the '43XX'), a siding and connecting line to the LMS and the two lines and platforms of that company's station; it was removed during the 1936–39 rebuilding scheme.

The Northern Line was invariably the last of the company's main routes to receive new locomotives, and the 4-4-0 'Counties' were not allocated to Stafford Road shed until August 1908, some four years after their introduction. Nevertheless, some examples from Old Oak shed were to be seen on Birkenhead trains before that time, with No. 3475 recorded at Leamington on 24th July 1906. By the latter 1920s, the class were largely working on secondary express and local turns, and on the northern route these included through trains to and from the south coast. In this view, No. 3819 *County of Salop* (from Tyseley) is believed to have been at the head of the 11.05 a.m. Wolverhampton to Weymouth service at Leamington in September 1928. Leamington shed itself also had a 'County' at this time for the morning train to Birkenhead.

Leamington shed traditionally provided an engine for banking duties on the four-mile climb from Warwick to Hatton, assisting goods trains on the ten-minute run to the level section there; much of the climb could be carried out on the 2½-mile long down goods loop between Budbrook and Hatton, thus releasing the down main for faster traffic. The banking turn, which also included shunting at Warwick and Hatton goods, lasted for twenty-four hours, with engines being changed at 6.00 a.m. '322' (Beyer') class 0-6-0 No. 354 is pictured here in the down bay at Warwick station in July 1934 on the banking turn, just one month before her withdrawal. She spent the last thirty or so years of her career in the Wolverhampton division, and most of that from 1914 at Leamington; No. 354 was the last survivor of her class, the penultimate engine having been withdrawn in 1931.

HATTON to TYSELEY

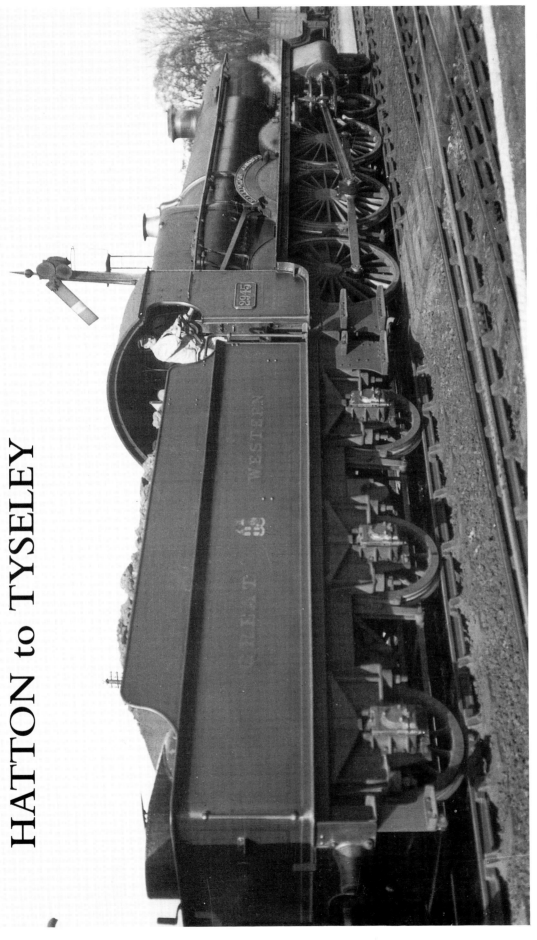

'Saint' class 4-6-0 No. 2945 *Hillingdon Court* alongside the up platform at Hatton station during 1934 with the 4.05 p.m. from Snow Hill to Paddington. From around 1910, a pair of expresses left Birmingham for London at around 4.00 p.m., the first calling at Leamington and then running non-stop to Paddington (via Bicester), the second serving (or slipping at) principal stations (via Oxford) en route. During the interwar period, the basis of both trains was the 2.05 p.m. Shrewsbury, which arrived at Snow Hill at 3.43 p.m. There, two carriages were removed from the front and attached to a six-coach set (including a dining car), which departed at 3.55 behind a Stafford Road 'King' for Leamington and Paddington (via Bicester). The remaining six vehicles were strengthened with a Third and a buffet car, and set off from Snow Hill at 4.05 p.m., with 'Star', 'Hall' or 'Saint' the more usual motive power. This train called at Hatton, Warwick, Leamington, Banbury, Oxford (where a four-coach section from Worcester was attached to the front), Reading, Ealing (to set down only) and Paddington, with a scheduled arrival of 7.28 p.m., about ninety minutes behind the direct train. The train engine stopped overnight at Old Oak shed, returning the following morning with the 6.30 a.m. to Wolverhampton.

'Hatton, Junction for Bearley, Alcester & Stratford-on-Avon'. In this 1934 view, the station is seen from the down platform, looking south, with the old Hatton South box in the distance. At this time, there were two boxes at the station, with Hatton Middle situated to the north of the station in the fork of the main and Stratford lines; both were replaced in January 1937 by a new South box, located on the down platform at about the position from which this photograph was taken. The new box contained 75 levers, having replaced the 31- and 55-lever frames of the South and Middle boxes respectively. Most of the Stratford branch trains ran through to or from Leamington, though a platform face (on the right) was provided for the services. The down goods loop from Budbrook ran in front of the old South box, with a connection to the down main at that point, although it was extended into the Stratford platform loop line with a further connection onto the down main to the north of the station.

Situated two miles to the north of Hatton, Rowington Junction was the point at which the 3½-mile Henley-in-Arden branch left the main line. In 1914, the route was served by auto cars working from Henley to Lapworth, some 1½ miles to the north of the junction, but trains were withdrawn during the Great War, and the central part of the route lifted to recover the rails. Rowington Junction box can be seen in the centre of this view, which was taken in the early 1930s, looking south, with the up home signal in the foreground. By this time, the truncated part of the branch was used for storage of wagons, a number of which can be seen in the distance on the right. The 560-yard Rowington troughs were located about the bridge in the distance on a short, level section of the route at the bottom of the 'dip' between Hatton summit and Lapworth.

ROWINGTON

'Saint' 4-6-0 No. 2928 *Saint Sebastian* approaching Rowington Junction with an up express in the early 1930s. As were the 4-4-0 'Counties' before them, the 'Saints' had been largely relegated to secondary express and local services on the Northern line by this time. Their duties now included such trains as the Birkenhead & Deal, the 4.35 p.m. Birkenhead to Paddington (via Oxford), and excursions onto the Southern Railway. Built in 1907, *Saint Sebastian* started her career at Exeter, and subsequently spent periods at Old Oak, Newport, Landore, Fishguard, Carmarthen, Oxford, Stafford Road, Shrewsbury and Chester, finishing her days at Westbury. She ran with a 3,500 gallon tender throughout her working life, and was withdrawn from service in August 1948, being scrapped in December of that year.

'28XX' class 2-8-0 No. 2878 from Tyseley shed with a down goods (probably bound for Bordesley Junction) in September 1931, held at the Rowington down starting signal, to the north of the junction. At this time, the '28XX' duties on the line included the 2.55 a.m. Bordesley to Southall coal, returning the next day with the 4.00 a.m. Southall to Bordesley goods and coal empties, and the 5.15 p.m. Bordesley to Old Oak coal, returning with the 2.45 p.m. Acton to Tyseley empties. It is possible that No. 2878 was pictured here on the 4.00 a.m. Southall, which was scheduled to convey up to 78 vehicles northwards from Banbury.

An Old Oak Common 'King', No. 6001 *King Edward VII*, approaching Rowington Junction with an up express in September 1931. This train was almost certainly the 11.45 a.m. Birkenhead to Paddington, the return working from Wolverhampton for the engine' of the 9.10 a.m. Paddington to Birkenhead, normally the only Northern line service hauled daily by an Old Oak 'King'. The train's scheduled formation at this point was a Van Third and Compo from Aberystwyth, a 70ft Brake Compo from Pwllheli, with a Dining Car and a four-coach 70ft rake (Van Third, Compo, Third, Van Third) from Birkenhead, although these were sometimes strengthened with extra vehicles from Wolverhampton. Leaving Birmingham (Snow Hill) at 3.00 p.m., this 'Luncheon and Tea Car Train' called at Leamington Spa and Banbury en route to Paddington (via Bicester) for a 5.05 p.m. arrival.

BENTLEY HEATH

Bentley Heath crossing was situated about half-a-mile to the north of Knowle & Dorridge station, and ten miles from Snow Hill. In this view, 'Star' class 4-6-0 No. 4031 *Queen Mary* is seen with the 11.15 a.m. Wolverhampton to Weymouth train, a few hundred yards to the north of the crossing, c.1932. The coach formation was that for the summer months, with a Brake Van, Third, Compo, Third and Van Third specified; during the winter timetable, the leading Brake Van and Third were replaced by a Van Third, presumably due to a lesser demand for seating and luggage space. A service of through coaches between Wolverhampton and Weymouth was introduced around the turn of the century, being expanded into a through train after the Great War. At Bank Holiday periods, the service was strengthened by up to five extra coaches, and in the August holiday was often run in two parts, with the main train consisting of twelve vehicles.

In the early 1930s, Tyseley shed housed seven '28XX' 2-8-0s for heavy goods turns between Bordesley and London. In addition to the two up coal trains and returning empties each day, the engines also ran the 10.55 a.m. Bordesley to Southall coal and goods, returning with the 3.13 p.m. Southall to Bordesley goods. Here No. 2875, from Tyseley, is seen heading southwards with a class 'H' goods, possibly the 10.55 a.m. Bordesley, c.1932. The quadrupling of the line was well under way, although the new trackwork had yet to be ballasted; when completed, the lines (from the right) were up and down main, up and down relief. Although the new arrangements between Olton and Lapworth were brought into operation in May 1933, it is believed that the nearest line (down relief) was used as a down goods loop between Bentley Heath and Widney Manor for a few months prior to that.

33

Bentley Heath Crossing box, c.1930, situated on the south side of the crossing to the east (up side) of the line. This picture was taken prior to the start of quadrupling of the 8¼-mile section between Olton and Lapworth. This was in effect a continuation of previous work in which relief lines had been provided between Birmingham (Moor Street) and Olton in the years before the Great War. The scheme was authorised under the 1929 Development (Loans, Guarantees and Grants) Act, under which the Great Western started thirty-four works of varying magnitude, in cooperation with the Government, for the relief of unemployment. Up and down goods running loops were provided between Bentley Heath and Knowle station, each able to house an engine, 105 wagons and a brake van. Opened c.1875, the box housed fifteen levers and the gear for the crossing gates, which was being held by the signalman in this view.

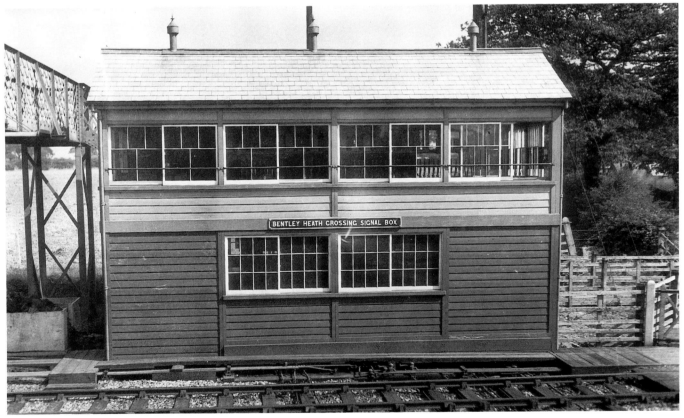

The new Bentley Heath Crossing box, opened in 1932 as the quadrupling neared completion. Situated on the same side of the line as the old box, but positioned to the north of the crossing, it was a considerably larger structure, housing 49 levers to accommodate the extra signalling and pointwork functions on the new running lines, and the wheel for the larger gates (just visible inside the box at the right-hand end). A pedestrian footbridge was provided immediately to the north of the box, with steps to its rear, to enable the public to cross safely over the four running lines, displacing, it is believed, the original wicket gates. The up and down goods refuge loops were reinstated between Knowle station and Bentley Heath, one on each side of the quadruple running lines, but with a reduced capacity (down, 89 wagons; up, 80 wagons).

WIDNEY MANOR

Widney Manor, looking south from the station with two down trains approaching, c.1934. On the down main, '51XX' class 2-6-2T No. 5144 from Stourbridge Junction shed was running with what might have been a set of corridor coaches from one of the mixed London to Worcester trains. At this time, the 9.45 a.m. Paddington to Wolverhampton (via Worcester) train also conveyed a through section for Birmingham, which was detached at Oxford, and forwarded thence as a semi-fast. On the right, '43XX' 2-6-0 No. 8300 can be seen approaching on the down relief line with a 'C' class (vacuum) goods. From 1933, this engine was allocated to Tyseley, Stafford Road and Oxley, and must have been a familiar sight in the area. Having previously carried the number 5300 (to 1927), she was renumbered back again during 1944, along with the vast majority of the '83s'.

Widney Manor, looking north from the down platform in 1931. The station was a latecomer to the Birmingham area, being opened in July 1899 to serve the surrounding district, and was provided with the usual rural station facilities including cattle pens and loading dock. In the early 1930s, Widney Manor was a minor part of the suburban network, with about half (twelve) of the local trains running between Leamington, Lapworth or Knowle and Snow Hill in each direction calling at the station. Staff at this time consisted of a station master, one porter and two signalmen.

'Aberdare' 2-6-0 No. 2632 passing through the old Widney Manor station during the spring of 1931 with an up empty stock train, carrying 'D' lamps on the tender. A Pontypool Road engine at this time, No. 2632 was a long way from home, though she had spent a couple of years at Leamington before being transferred to the Welsh shed in 1930. It was quite unusual to see such engines on passenger stock trains, but not unknown. Perhaps she was being repositioned for her next goods turn, and a convenient task was found to avoid light engine mileage; or perhaps a suitable mixed traffic engine was not available for the working, and the visiting '26XX' was utilised.

Something which always created a great deal of interest amongst enthusiasts was the eight-wheel, 3,500-gallon tender No. 1755, built for the *Great Bear* in February 1908 (Dia. A76). It was rather heavy, weighing some 23½ tons tare, five tons more than contemporary 3,500 tenders. After the demise of the *Bear* in 1924, the tender was attached to 4-4-0 'Counties', 'Saints' and 'Stars', before being withdrawn in 1936. On 16th January 1933, the tender was attached to 'Saint' class 4-6-0 No. 2916 *Saint Benedict* at Chester, and running with the engine until January 1935, is pictured here at Widney Manor in 1934 on an evening train to Leamington, where the engine was based.

The quadrupling work at Widney Manor was well under way by the late summer of 1932, with excavations to accommodate the two new relief lines seen on the left. A new bridge was also required to carry the relief lines across the road at the northern end of the platforms, construction of which began shortly after this photograph was taken; the bridge was in partial use by November of that year, carrying a new down goods loop between Bentley Heath and the northern limits of the Widney Manor layout. The station yard was served daily by the 8.25 a.m. Bordesley to Oxford and the 10.15 a.m. Leamington to Tyseley local goods trains, with each scheduled to spend about ten minutes in the sidings.

'Hall' class 4-6-0 No. 4935 *Ketley Hall* approaching Widney Manor with an up express, c.1932. This engine spent her early years at Chester and Wolverhampton sheds, and although the 'Halls' were frequently to be seen on passenger services within the Wolverhampton division, they were utilised far more on goods duties. This was especially the case for those at Oxley shed, where No. 4935 was allocated for a period. Apart from one short spell, she was coupled to 3,500 gallon tenders until 1938, including two examples of 'Intermediate' tenders in the early and mid 'thirties. *Ketley Hall* moved to Old Oak Common in April 1936.

The signal box at Widney Manor, pictured in 1931, before the work on quadrupling began. This box was worked in two shifts, opening at 6.45 a.m. and closing 8.45 p.m. each weekday, and was switched out overnight and on Sundays; it housed 27 levers in 1944.

'Castle' class 4-6-0 No. 4080 *Powderham Castle* nearing Solihull station with the 9.05 a.m. Birkenhead to Paddington during the summer of 1927, a train which ran in connection with the overnight Belfast to Liverpool steamer. In addition to the engine change at Wolverhampton, the six-vehicle train was strengthened by a further four coaches, including a three-car articulated dining set to create the advertised 'Luncheon Car Train'. No. 4080 was a Laira engine at this time, but it was not unknown for West Country locomotives to find their way onto the Northern line duties, utilised by Old Oak shed. The two T. H. Truelove & Sons wagons amongst the selection of opens on the coal siding belonged to a local merchant.

SOLIHULL

Solihull was one of the more important intermediate stations on the section between Birmingham and Leamington, opened along with the mixed gauge route between Oxford and Birmingham in October 1852. This view was taken from the down platform, looking south, c.1927, with the broad gauge origins evident in the spacing of the main lines. At that time the station master at Solihull was responsible for a staff of thirteen — six at the passenger station, four at the goods shed, and three signalmen. The original station building, constructed in the 'chalet' style, was situated at the far end of the up platform, and had been joined, over the years, by a considerable number of other structures, swept away in the rebuilding of 1932.

The signal box at Solihull (its second) was situated on the up platform. Opened around August 1890 to replace the original structure at the south end of the down platform, the box contained 29 levers. Solihull cabin was opened continuously throughout the week, but closed at 6.00 a.m. on Sunday mornings for 24 hours.

Solihull's third signal box was opened in July 1932. Situated on the west side of the new station, the box was aligned with the top of the embankment, hence the very unusual lead-off arrangement. It was not common practice to position a large brick box on the side of made-up ground in this manner, but circumstances dictated otherwise. To control the considerable increase in facilities at Solihull, the new box contained 74 levers. This picture shows signalman George Horsley looking out from his new box, one of three men who manned the box each day.

George Horsley once more, pictured in the new box in 1933. In 1939, the new box remained open continuously throughout the week until 1.00 p.m. on Sundays, though it reopened between 6.0 and 11.45 p.m. on that day to deal with crossings between the main and relief lines, and a late-night terminating service. Solihull opened again at 5.00 a.m. on Monday mornings for the week's business. The levers were positioned for up main (0–6) and up relief signals (9–12) at the far (north) end of the box, and down relief (61–66) and main (69–74) signals at the near end.

TYSELEY

Tyseley shed was opened in 1908, replacing the shed at Bordesley, which had been demolished to permit the expansion of the Junction yards. From the adjacent Warwick Road, it was possible to get a good view of engines parked on sidings at the rear of the shed, as in this view of Old Oak's '47XX' class 2-8-0 No. 4705 in 1933. Old Oak '47XX' engines alternated with Tyseley's own allocation (two) on the 11.05 p.m. Paddington and 12.10 a.m. Park Royal vacuum goods, returning with the 8.20 p.m. Birkenhead and 10.35 p.m. Langley Green services.

After a couple of years at Old Oak shed when new, 'Hall' class No. 4971 *Stanway Hall* was transferred to the Wolverhampton division during September 1932, where she remained until 1947. Between April 1934 and February 1936 she was a Tyseley engine, with passenger and goods duties on both the Hereford and North Warwicks routes.

Another view of *Stanway Hall* at Tyseley, c.1933. This engine was one of the eleven 'Halls' to be modified to oil burning in 1947, running as No. 3901. On completion during May 1947, she was rostered on the 7.50 a.m. Taunton as between Swindon and Paddington, and later in that month was transferred to Laira, where she started on the 9.15 a.m. North Road to Penzance passenger, returning with the 1.25 p.m. Penzance to Paddington train. The engine was converted back to coal burning in April 1949.

THE NORTH WARWICKSHIRE LINE

YARDLEY WOOD

Yardley Wood Platform was situated on the North Warwicks line, 2½ miles to the south of the junction with the Northern line at Tyseley, and six miles from Snow Hill. Opened to passenger traffic in July 1908, Yardley Wood was provided with two platforms, a compact station building with the normal booking, waiting rooms and lavatories on the up side, and a small shelter on the down. Being in the 2½ mile section between Hall Green and Shirley 'boxes, there was no signal box there, but it was nevertheless a busy location, manned in the 'twenties by a station master and three porters (reduced to two in the 'thirties). In this view, the station is seen from the down platform, looking north towards Birmingham, c.1930.

SHIRLEY

Just over a mile to the south of Yardley stood the rather more significant station of Shirley. This picture shows 'County' class 4-4-0 No. 3816 *County of Leicester*, from Bristol (Bath Road) shed approaching the station in September 1930 with the four-coach 6.50 a.m. Taunton to Birmingham express. At this time, the engine was paired with the eight-wheel, 3,500 gallon tender from the *Great Bear*. Withdrawal of the 'County' class began in 1930, and No. 3816 went in September 1931, just twelve months after this photograph was taken.

Shirley, again in September 1930, looking north towards Birmingham, illustrating the substantial passenger buildings on each platform. Goods traffic commenced on the North Warwicks line in December 1907, with passenger services being introduced in the following July. Goods facilities included a shed, with cattle pens and a loading dock on the same road, and two mileage sidings to the rear. There were also two refuge sidings (one up and one down) for goods trains, one on each side of the station layout, and each capable of holding a train of around sixty wagons. In 1930, the passenger station was manned by a staff of five, with a goods porter and a motor driver in the yard.

The signal box at Shirley was located on the down (southbound) platform, towards its northern end, and housed 31 levers. Opened each morning for traffic at 5.30 a.m., the box was worked by two shifts of signalmen, plus a period by a porter/signalman from the station. The day's work ended at 12.15 a.m., when the box was switched out, and the section was thereafter controlled between Tyseley and Earlswood Lakes boxes.

Grimes Hill & Wythall station was situated two miles to the south of Shirley (9¼ miles from Snow Hill), and is seen here in 1931, looking south towards Stratford. Throughout its history, Grimes Hill was blessed with a number of different titles in the public timetables: in 1912 it was shown as Grimes Hill Platform, Grimes Hill & Wythall Halt in 1922, Grimes Hill & Wythall Platform in 1926, with the 'Platform' suffix being dropped around 1933. The station became Wythall in the 'seventies. Facilities were basic, with a booking office at road level, and waiting room and lavatories on the platforms. The 5¾ milepost (from Tyseley) can be seen at the near edge of the nearer 'pagoda' building. Grimes Hill had its own station master in the 'twenties (assisted by a porter), but was manned by two porters thereafter, coming under the control of Earlswood Lakes.

Carrying an 'A' head code, 'Bulldog' 4-4-0 No. 3321 *Brasenose* was photographed to the north of Earlswood Lakes at the head of 5.00 p.m. semi-fast Birmingham to Stratford, c.1933. Built in November 1899, *Brasenose* was one of the first batch of twenty engines with curved frames, a feature shared with the twenty converted 'Dukes' (1902–09), and the first of the class to appear, No. 3340 *Camel*. Along with many of her sister engines, No. 3321 spent her early years in the West Country, with several years at Weymouth on the London trains before moving to Swindon in 1909. She was later transferred to Oxford (1916) and Reading (1921), finally moving into the Wolverhampton division in 1924. *Brasenose* was withdrawn in 1935.

EARLSWOOD LAKES

The '30XX' ROD 2-8-0s first came into Great Western hands on sale and on hire from the Government in 1919, with the first twenty being taken into stock by the company, and the other eighty-four eventually returning to Government control in 1921/2. Amongst the former group was No. 3014, seen here in the down refuge siding to the north of Earlswood Lakes station c.1931 with what is believed to be the 9.25 a.m. Bordesley to Swindon class 'H' goods, running via Gloucester. The engine was from Westbury shed, and was probably taking this scheduled return working to the previous day's 4.40 a.m. Westbury (ex-Tavistock Junction; 10.10 a.m. Swindon) to Bordesley service. The train carried traffic for Swindon, Taunton (and branches), Exeter, Newton Abbot and beyond, and called at Gloucester to pick up.

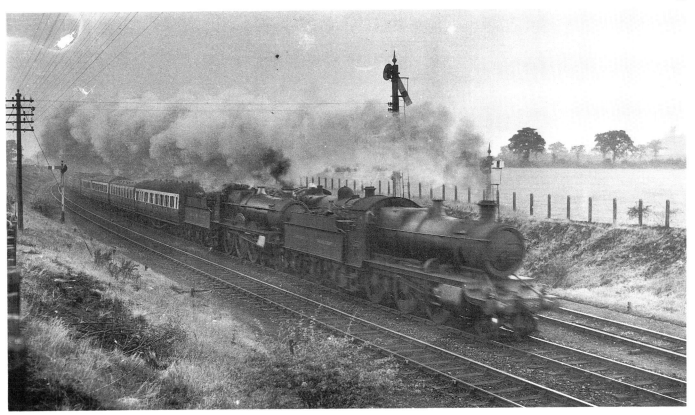

With No. 3014 and her train safely housed in the refuge siding, the road was clear for the 10.25 Birmingham to Weston-super-Mare express, which is believed to have been the train featured in the photograph. This normally comprised six coaches, but was strengthened during peak periods. The train engine was Tyseley's 'Saint' No. 2906 *Lady of Lynn*, assisted by '43XX' No. 6339, from Chester shed; it was not unusual to find engines from distant sheds being used on express trains between their normal goods duties during the summer months, which may have been the case with No. 6339 in this instance. In the early 1930s, 'Saints' and 'Halls' ran most of the regular express services on the North Warwicks line, though 'Stars' appeared occasionally. By the mid 1930s, 'Castles' had been introduced onto the Wolverhampton & Penzance services, working through to and from Plymouth.

Earlswood Lakes station, looking north, c.1931. Some ten miles from Snow Hill, the station served 'a very favourite resort for those wishing to enjoy the beautiful lanes of leafy Warwickshire. The reservoirs of the Stratford-on-Avon Canal form a very picturesque sheet of water backed by wooded slopes', according to the 1923 edition of *Holiday Haunts*. In the early 1930s, Earlswood Lakes was served daily by about ten terminating/originating trains, as well as around twenty local services in each direction between Moor Street and Henley, Bearley or Stratford. The Station Master at Earlswood had three porters to assist him, plus three signalmen for the 24-hour box, situated at the south end of the station on the up side. The station was at the summit of a ten-mile climb from Bearley (North).

'Saint' class 4-6-0 No. 2908 *Lady of Quality* approaching Danzey station with an up West of England express for Birmingham, c.1931. Stationed at Bath Road, No. 2908 may have been hauling the 2.20 p.m. Bristol to Wolverhampton train, conveying through vehicles from Penzance and Kingswear, with a return trip scheduled on the 6.35 p.m. Birmingham to Bristol and Taunton express.

HENLEY-IN-ARDEN

On Monday, 9th July 1934, an express railcar service between Birmingham, Gloucester and Cardiff was inaugurated, using Cars Nos. 2–4. Advertised as 'Streamlined Luxury Rail Cars', the units were equipped with a buffet at one end, two lavatories, and seated 44 passengers. Two return journeys were scheduled, the 116-mile trips taking just under 2½ hours. One of the cars, with buffet end trailing, is seen here passing Henley-in-Arden station c.1935 with the 9.05 a.m. Snow Hill to Cardiff service. The small market town had two stations, the first of which was a terminus, served by a branch from Rowington Junction. The terminus was closed to passenger services in 1908, when the North Warwick line opened, but continued in use as a goods depot until the 1960s. From 1908, auto services from Lapworth over the branch used the new station, utilising a new link line, which can just be seen beyond the bridge in the distance. The branch was closed to passenger services during the Great War, and mostly lifted, though the link remained for access to the old terminus, for goods purposes.

Taken around 6.40 p.m. on a late summer's evening in 1929, this picture shows Stafford Road 'Saint' No. 2917 *Saint Bernard* climbing the bank between Wootton Wawen and Henley-in-Arden with the 10.30 a.m. Penzance to Wolverhampton express. The regular train comprised a five-coach section (including a dining car) from Penzance, two vehicles from Kingswear, and a Brake Compo from Weston-super-Mare, with strengthening when required. The peak summer service also conveyed vehicles to and from Newquay. This service commenced with the opening of the line in 1908, providing a daily through connection between the Midlands and the West Country. 'Saint' class engines replaced the 'County' and other 4-4-0s on the more important North Warwick line services in the latter 1920s, though they were soon joined by 'Halls' and 'Stars'. From the early 'thirties, 'Castles' took over the main West of England trains, running through from Wolverhampton to Newton Abbott or Plymouth; they were to be regularly found on the 'Penzance' service until the 1960s.

THE STRATFORD BRANCH
CLAVERDON

Claverdon was the only intermediate station on the 5½-mile line between Bearley and Hatton Junctions, a useful connecting route between the North Warwick and main Northern lines. The station pictured here was the original, opened by the Stratford-on-Avon Railway Company in October 1860, on the Hatton & Stratford route, with a single running line and a goods siding. During the late 'thirties, the line through Claverdon was doubled, and a new station with two platforms was built to the west of the old site.

BEARLEY

Bearley station, c.1935, looking east towards Hatton. The 4½-mile single line section through Claverdon to Hatton Branch Junction commenced at the far end of the platforms, and by the 1930s was the cause of some operating inconvenience. Modifications to the station carried out on the doubling of the line, completed in 1939, included the lengthening of the platforms to 450ft (up) and 550ft (down), the rebuilding of the small waiting room/station master's office on the down platform (right), and the provision of a steel footbridge between the platforms.

'Bulldog' 4-4-0 No. 3449 *Nightingale*, on a Worcester to Leamington fast goods, waiting at Bearley East Junction box for the passing of a down train to Stratford through the single line section, c.1933. The engine was allocated to Worcester shed between 1931 and 1936, and records show that the eight 'Bulldogs' there were utilised on both goods and passenger turns. After her stay at Worcester, *Nightingale* moved to Laira, where she was recorded assisting passenger trains to Newton Abbot, Penzance and Newquay, and running relief trains to Truro. She returned to the Gloucester and Cheltenham area in 1938, working on both the M & SWJ and Hereford lines, ending her days at Swindon in 1951.

THE ALCESTER BRANCH

Aston Cantlow Halt, on the Alcester branch, looking west towards Alcester c.1940. The 6½-mile branch was opened for traffic in September 1876, though Aston Cantlow was not erected until December 1922, located about two miles from Bearley station, a short distance to the north of the village it served. The halt was closed in September 1939, though an unadvertised workmen's service between Leamington, Warwick, Aston Cantlow and Great Alne operated during the war, with an auto engine and trailer stabled at Leamington. After the Second World War, a full service between Stratford, Bearley and Alcester appeared in the service timetables, though with the inscription 'Service Suspended' below, reflecting the announcement carried in the public timetables.

The Alcester branch was worked mostly from Bearley station, though one train daily (three on Saturdays) ran through to Stratford-on-Avon, some of which avoided Bearley. From its early days, the branch was the preserve of '517' class engines. Around the turn of the century, No. 1444 was recorded on trains in 1898/9, and Nos. 1156, 1430 and 1484 in 1901/2, with stock in the first decade of the century specified as an 8-wheel Brake Compo and a 4-wheel Van. The line closed during the Great War, but reopened just after the Grouping, with auto-trailers in use. During 1933, a new '48XX' tank (No. 4814) appeared at Alcester, and alternated with the '517s' until the last of the latter class was transferred away during 1935. This picture shows '517' class 0–4–2T No. 564 approaching Alcester Branch Junction c.1933 with a Bearley train, just a few months before her withdrawal. Engines sometimes took water at the aqueduct near the Branch Junction at Bearley, with two minutes being allowed in the timetable to permit this operation.

HONEYBOURNE

Honeybourne station, looking west along the main lines towards Worcester in 1935. The station was rebuilt during the early years of this century in conjunction with the opening of the new Birmingham & Bristol route, which passed under the main Oxford & Worcester line about three-quarters of a mile to the east. In addition to the main lines (served by platforms 1 and 2), there was a pair of branch/relief lines to the north, seen on the right (platforms 3 and 4), which were connected by double junctions with the mains to allow trains to or from any direction to use any appropriate platform. The traffic through Honeybourne station was diverse, ranging from the Paddington, Worcester & Hereford expresses, the Leamington, Stratford, Evesham & Worcester locals, to the Cheltenham auto-trains, with a wide selection of goods services, including the South Wales & Yarnton (Oxford) mineral trains.

A member of the '2361' series of outside-frame 'Dean Goods', No. 2380, is pictured on the siding to the rear (north) of platform No. 4 on shunting duties in 1935. This engine (alternating with others of the series) was sub-shedded at Honeybourne from Worcester for periods during the 'thirties, and employed on banking and shunting duties, a turn for which the more powerful '2361s' were favoured throughout the interwar years. The duty was also worked by the '2301' class, but was eventually taken over by '2251' locomotives. No. 2380 moved on into Wales during 1939, being withdrawn from service in 1943.

The ultimate 'Dean Goods', No. 2580, standing on the up relief line at the west end of Honeybourne station in 1935 with a local 'K' class goods train, probably the morning train to Cheltenham and Gloucester (where the engine was based). The '2301' engines were a very familiar sight at Honeybourne, with examples from Worcester and Tyseley also visiting daily on local goods turns at this time. No. 2580 was taken over by the War Department in 1939 for the second time in her career, and went to France again during the following year; this time, she did not reappear.

Pontypool Road '28XX' 2-8-0 No. 2824 moving off the up goods loop onto the up relief, and running through Honeybourne station with a class 'F' goods train, in 1935. The service might have been the 3.00 a.m. Pontypool Road to Oxford, which was scheduled for '28XX' haulage, although the headlamps should have been changed from 'F' to 'J' at Worcester. At this time, the through goods traffic between South Wales and Oxford was limited, although it expanded considerably during and after the war, most especially in coal and ore. Trains were routed either via Hereford or via Gloucester, the latter reversing at Honeybourne. The banking engine would be available at Honeybourne to assist the trains up the bank to Campden or Moreton-in-Marsh, depending upon the load, train engine power, and the traffic situation beyond Blockley.

The passenger service between Honeybourne and Cheltenham opened in five stages between 1904 and 1906, and was worked by steam railmotors. From the mid-1920s, auto-trains from Cheltenham and Gloucester alternated on the duties, though by the late 1920s, the autos were dominant. Two trailers were specified for each train in 1929, though by 1937 this had been reduced to one, but with two at times of peak traffic. It was customary after the Great War for a small number of the trains to run through between Cheltenham and Evesham, and the first departure from Cheltenham continued to do that into the 'fifties. The auto-trains were initially worked by '517s', though in 1932 the '48XXs' appeared on the scene, with Gloucester, Cheltenham (and Chalford) taking the first five new engines from Swindon works. No. 4813 is seen here on the up branch road (platform No. 4) with a late morning Cheltenham train (probably the 11.13 a.m. from Honeybourne) in 1935, coupled to trailer No. 32; she was delivered when new to Gloucester in March 1933, and remained in the district until her withdrawal in March 1956.

'Hall' class 4-6-0 No. 4918 *Dartington Hall* from Tyseley shed waiting at Honeybourne's up main platform with an express, during 1935. The '7XX' code carried on the smokebox door identified a Wolverhampton division to West Country train, though in 1934, the first year of the codes, these trains had been numbered in the '3XX' series. In this instance, train No. 725 is believed to have been the Saturdays-only 9.35 a.m. Smethwick Jct to Weston-super-Mare (which carried code No. 720 from 1936 onwards, from when the '7XX' number series stabilised until the outbreak of war). The train was routed via Stourbridge Jct and Worcester, calling at Honeybourne at 11.23 a.m., running thence via Cheltenham and Bristol. Curiously, the return train (5.10 p.m. Weston) did not call at Honeybourne, and passengers had to travel back from Evesham.

An up stopping train waiting alongside No. 2 platform, Honeybourne, behind 'Star' 4-6-0 No. 4049 *Princess Maud*, during the summer of 1935. This was probably the 8.23 a.m. Wolverhampton to Oxford (via Worcester) and Paddington, a four-coach train (plus Siphon G) which ran all stations to Oxford, with forty stops, in 4¾ hours. At Oxford, it was strengthened by four more vehicles (including a Dining Car), before running on as a 'Luncheon Car Train', calling at Didcot and Reading en route. *Princess Maud* was from Worcester, and was scheduled to return from Paddington with the 4.45 p.m. to Wolverhampton, a train which, in complete contrast to the up journey, ran non-stop to Oxford, then called only at Moreton-in-Marsh and Evesham on the way back to Worcester. The engine would spend nine hours on the road working this turn from and to her home shed.

KINGHAM

Kingham, c.1930, looking along the main lines towards Oxford. This station was opened in August 1855 as Chipping Norton Junction, along with the 4½-mile branch north-eastwards to Chipping Norton, some two years after that part of the Oxford, Worcester & Wolverhampton line on which it stood. In March 1863, the branch westwards to Bourton-on-the-Water was opened for traffic, and later extended into Cheltenham in June 1881. The last portion of what had become the Banbury & Cheltenham Direct Railway was opened between King's Sutton (3½ miles south of Banbury) and Chipping Norton, making the Junction truly a crossroads of some importance. At this time, the station was served by main line trains on the Oxford and Worcester route, local trains from Oxford, and those between Banbury and Cheltenham. The main building, on the down main platform (right), housed the booking office, waiting room, ladies waiting room and lavatory, station master's office, gentlemen's lavatory, and the porter's room, and was constructed in yellow brick with blue dressing. The bridge beyond the station carried the road between Chipping Norton and Stow-in-the-Wold. At this time, Kingham had a staff of fifteen for the station and yard, and six signalmen for the Station, East and West boxes.

In this view, the station is seen from the opposite end of the central island platform, looking down the main lines towards Worcester, c.1930. The name was changed to Kingham in 1909, possibly to avoid any confusion caused by the similar title to Chipping Norton itself, but perhaps also to reflect the increase in places served by branch lines from the station since the original name was bestowed. There was a small refreshment room on the island platform around the time of the Great War (visible here in the foreground), but it had ceased to operate by the early 'thirties. The substantial footbridge (two 44ft spans) served all four platforms, and also a footpath leading to the nearby Langston Arms Hotel. The station master's house can be seen on the extreme left-hand edge of the picture.

Looking north from the down main platform, Kingham, with the station box in the centre, c.1930. There were originally two boxes on the main line at Kingham; the South box, containing 33 levers, was situated off the south end of the island platform, against the road bridge, whilst the original North box was replaced by the structure seen above in July 1905. The South box was dispensed with (from 4th November 1922) and the levers were centralized in the North box, which then contained 91. To the right of the box, a '45XX' can be seen on the 44ft 9in turntable, positioned in front of the 1913 engine shed. An 0-6-0 tender engine was stationed here for early morning shunting, and for working the Cheltenham goods at around 10.15 a.m. The raised water tank on the right provided a supply for the column on the down main platform (left), and another at the south end of the up branch platform; the supply was apparently limited, and a working notice enjoined main line enginemen to obtain water elsewhere whenever possible, to ensure a good supply for the branch engines. The bridge in the distance carried the direct loop, avoiding Kingham; opened in 1906, this line was used daily by the Barry/Swansea & Newcastle expresses, and through goods trains between Banbury & Gloucester, plus others using it to position on the main lines (Banbury to Wolverhampton goods trains, 1914), or to reach the goods yard from the Banbury direction. The yard can be seen on the left.

The branch platforms at Kingham, looking north. Trains for Cheltenham would turn sharp left at the far end of the platform and cross the main lines to reach the branch, whilst those to Banbury turned right, passing in front of the water tower in the distance. By the 1930s, the Cheltenham trains were mostly '45XXs' and 'B' sets, whilst the Banbury services were '48XXs' or '54XXs' and an auto-trailer, in addition to which there were a small number of services running between Kingham and Chipping Norton.

Kingham, branch platforms, looking south towards Oxford. The three signals controlled departures from the 'Cheltenham' (right-hand) platform, for the Banbury (with the East box distant), Down Main and Cheltenham directions. The small shelter on the Banbury platform (left) also housed a gents lavatory, whilst the footbridge extension behind it towards the Langston Arms Hotel is clearly visible. Kingham's second water crane can be seen at the far end of the Banbury platform. The two buildings under the island platform canopy (right) housed the waiting and ladies waiting rooms, each with adjacent lavatories. It is sad to relate that, apart from two working platforms, this most attractive station has all but disappeared.

THE BANBURY & CHELTENHAM DIRECT

On 1st May 1906, the Great Western (in conjunction with the Great Central Railway) inaugurated a Cardiff & Newcastle service, with one train in each direction daily. The service was unusual in that, between Banbury and Gloucester, it took a distinctly non-express route, running over the Banbury & Cheltenham line; however this was a rather more direct path than would be afforded by the main line via Didcot, being some 16 miles shorter. The 42-mile section between King's Sutton and Hatherley Junction, Cheltenham, was relatively slow going, with 1hr 20mins scheduled, though this included an allowance for stops at Chipping Norton, Stow-on-the-Wold and Bourton-on-the-Water to set down passengers from the LNER, or to pick them up on the eastbound journey. This 1935 picture shows '43XX' No. 6352 (from Banbury) hauling the 9.30 a.m. Newcastle to Swansea up the gradient between Bourton-on-the-Water and Notgrove, three miles of which was at 1 in 60, nearing Notgrove. The train was of GWR stock, though with a strengthening LNER Brake Third.

Cheltenham's '4575' 2-6-2T No. 5524 climbing the bank towards Notgrove with the 2.22 p.m. Kingham to Cheltenham (St. James) in 1935. The branch stock for this train was a Van Third and a Third, but it also conveyed through coaches off the 12.45 p.m. Paddington to Hereford express, which called at Kingham to detach the Cheltenham Compo and Brake Third (corridor stock), which may be seen in the centre of the train. The remaining four daily return services between Cheltenham and Kingham were operated with a Compo and Van Third. The locomotive working on the services was more varied than might at first seem likely; Malvern Road's six '45XX' turns worked an intensive service between Cheltenham and Gloucester, with trips to Kingham rostered within. The engine seen above was detailed as coming off shed at 11.53 a.m., working the 12.10 p.m. to Kingham, the 2.22 p.m. return, then three return trips to Gloucester (including a return trip to Stroud on Thursdays and Saturdays), arriving back on shed at 1.20 a.m. the following morning. Up to four different engines were used on the branch passenger trains in the course of the day during the 1930s.

'43XX' No. 5321 from Banbury shed running down the bank between Notgrove and Bourton-on-the-Water with the 8.15 a.m. Swansea to Newcastle train, during 1936. The service started in 1906 running to and from Cardiff, but by 1907 had been extended to Barry, earning the unofficial title 'Ports-to-Ports Express'. The normal formation in the early years was five vehicles, including a dining car, advertised as a 'Luncheon and Tea Car Train'. After the Great War, the service was extended westwards to Swansea, departing there at 7.30 a.m., and presumably adding breakfast to the menu in the process. However, the service was for a time cut back again to Barry, though a through coach between Hull and Barry was added; by 1927, Swansea was again the destination, with five or six vehicles and the Hull Brake Compo. Each company operated one train, which was often strengthened on summer Fridays and Saturdays. The service via the B & CD line ceased in 1939, and when reintroduced in 1946, ran via Didcot.

The 8.15 a.m. Swansea to Newcastle with GWR stock, this time behind No. 6327, again from Banbury shed, c.1935. Through engine working between Banbury and Swansea (High St) on this service was introduced in the late 1920s, previous to which engines had been changed at Gloucester and Cardiff on the down journey, and at Cardiff on the up. Whilst Banbury engines and men generally worked through on the regular trains, Cardiff (Canton) locomotives and crews were involved when duplicates were run, and carried out a return trip to and from Banbury in the day. No. 6327 was a Banbury engine between 1933 and 1947, and worked on this train regularly until the class were displaced on the duty to some degree by the new 'Manors' in 1939.

To the north of Chedworth tunnel, trains on the ex-M&SWJ line passed through the sylvan setting of Chedworth Woods. In this view, ex-M & SW 4-4-0 No. 1124 is seen heading north towards Withington (Glos) on a Cheltenham service, probably the 2.40 p.m. from Andover Junction, c.1934. No. 1124 was withdrawn from service in August 1935, after a working life of only 25 years, and spent much of her Great Western career at Andover Junction shed. The normal coach formation of trains on the line comprised Van Third, Third, Brake Compo, seen here, though not in the order specified in the coach programme. Perhaps the train was easier to operate at stations with the van portions inboard.

THE MIDLAND & SOUTH WESTERN JUNCTION RAILWAY

'26XX' 2-6-0 No. 2626 from Cheltenham (High Street) shed in Chedworth Woods with a northbound local goods train, c.1934. This engine was transferred from Southall to the Gloucester district in 1933, where she remained until her withdrawal in April 1937. Nine engines of this class were transferred to Cheltenham and Gloucester in the early 1930s, and appeared regularly on the line, especially on the 8.10 a.m. Gloucester to Swindon Town 'pick-up', and the 2.15 p.m. return. They were used mostly on less demanding tasks, and for many the allocation was their last.

'Duke' class 4-4-0s appeared on the ex-M & SWJ line shortly after the grouping, and were to be seen on passenger services regularly until the war years. No. 3278 *Trefusis* is pictured here in Chedworth Woods with a northbound train, c.1935, again possibly the 2.40 p.m. Andover Junction. She was transferred from Tyseley in 1931, and spent most of her time at Andover Junction, being withdrawn in 1938. Gloucester shed retained a couple of the class until nationalization, though by that time they were being used mostly on goods turns, especially on the Kingham line.

A down local passenger train accelerating away from Dawlish Warren behind '45XX' 2-6-2T No. 4531, c.1935. The leading vehicle of this varied rake was auto-trailer No. 201, converted from steam railmotor No. 69 in 1934. Like many of her class, No. 4531 spent her entire working life in the Newton Abbot division, and was the first '45XX' to be withdrawn, in February 1950. The engine was pictured here under Langstone Cliff, just prior to running alongside the sea wall for the mile to Dawlish station.

THE WEST COUNTRY

DAWLISH

Looking north from Langstone Rock, showing the estuary of the River Exe, with Dawlish Warren station in the distance. The first Warren station was situated at the northern end of the trackwork curve in the foreground, near to the public footbridge, but was replaced in 1912 by that just visible beyond. This was at one time a notorious smugglers' haunt, but became popular as a site for picnics, and had an eighteen-hole golf course along the north side of the Warren. Evidence of the never-ending battle with the sea can be seen in the foreground with the renewal of defences, using large rocks.

'Castle' class 4-6-0 No. 5027 *Farleigh Castle* passing the down home signal at Dawlish with an express, c.1935. This engine entered traffic in May 1934 at Old Oak Common, remaining at that shed for the whole of her Great Western career. In the January 1934 issue of the *GWR Magazine*, No. 5027 was detailed to carry the name *Exeter Castle*, with No. 5028 receiving *Farleigh*, though this was changed before either engine appeared from Swindon. The train was the 10.25 a.m. from Paddington to Falmouth, which in 1935 also conveyed through coaches to Helston. Although a short-lived feature of the 10.25, the Helston through coaches were reintroduced before the war. On summer Saturdays in that year, the 10.25 a.m. was the first of four trains leaving Paddington at five-minute intervals for the West Country, including the 'Cornish Riviera Limited' and 'The Cornishman', with coaches for Weymouth, Newquay, Falmouth, St. Ives and Penzance conveyed variously by the other three.

'Bulldog' 4-4-0 No. 3443 *Chaffinch*, seen here in the coach sidings at Newton Abbot, was resident at that shed between 1931 and 1935. In addition to local and pilot work, No. 3443 was recorded on banking duties from Newton. During July 1932, she was used to assist the down 'Riviera' to Plymouth, returning to Newton on the 1.30 p.m. Penzance to Paddington train. *Chaffinch* was also recorded on the 9.30 a.m. Paddington as far as Brent in August 1934, and on the down 'Riviera' to Plymouth, returning home on the 12.15 p.m. Penzance to Crewe. In general terms at this time, the 'Bulldogs' and '83XXs' were favoured for passenger banking between Newton and Plymouth, whilst the '3150' engines assisted passenger and goods trains, mostly to Totnes or Brent.

NEWTON ABBOT

Newton Abbot, c.1934, looking towards Plymouth from the down main platform. The station was rebuilt in 1927, with two island platforms serving the
main and relief lines, plus a bay (to the right of the picture) alongside the main
building on the up side for the Moretonhampstead services. Although there was
limited storage accommodation for coaches at Paignton and Kingswear, much of
the stock was brought back to Newton, and stored in the sidings on the left.
The water tank at the engine shed/factory can be seen on the extreme left of
the picture, whilst the wagon repair shops are in the centre, beyond the signal
gantry.

'28XX' class 2-8-0 No. 2854 waiting on the down through line at Newton Abbot, c.1935, with the wagon shops in the background. This engine was stationed at Laira, one of four at that shed, which seem to have been used largely on duties to and from Bristol, though a Swindon turn was also run. The restrictions imposed on loads over the South Devon banks can be judged from the fact that the '28XX' could haul just twenty loaded coal wagons unassisted up Dainton to the standard schedule, and twenty-two up Rattery; she could pull ninety along the section from Exeter to Newton.

Newton Abbot used one auto-train on its local services, running mainly to and from Moretonhampstead, though with trips to Totnes and Paignton included. '517' class 0-4-2T No. 1443 was a latecomer onto the auto scene, being so fitted in 1929 to work in the West Country. She is pictured here on the up relief line at Newton Abbot station, c.1934, possibly with the 5.35 p.m. Paignton to Moretonhampstead train. No. 1443 was withdrawn from service in December 1934, working largely on the Ashburton branch during the final months. Unlike Exeter, which had a number of auto units in operation daily, Newton did not receive any of the new '48XX' engines until 1936, soldiering on with her ageing '517s'.

The powerful lines of the 'King' class are evident in this portrait of Old Oak's No. 6009 *King Charles II*, standing on the down main at Newton station during the late afternoon, c.1932. The train could have been the 1.30 p.m. Paddington to Penzance, which had just seven regular vehicles to take on from Newton, and would not therefore normally require an assisting engine. The 'King' workings to and from the West Country varied somewhat over the years, but in the mid-1930s this engine returned the following day with through and local working as far as Taunton, where it picked up the 1.30 p.m. for Paddington.

'Castle' 4-6-0 No. 5011 *Tintagel Castle* from Newton Abbot shed standing at the up relief platform, Newton, in the spring of 1930. When new, No. 5011 was paired with a 4,000 gallon tender, but in January 1930 it was given a 3,500 gallon one, No. 2225, for a few months before reverting to the larger type. It was the practice to mark the shed code on the engine lamps at this time, and the letters 'NA' may just be discerned on the nearer of the pair. During the late 'twenties/early 'thirties, Newton Abbot shed worked the 8.35 a.m. Plymouth to Paddington train onwards from Exeter, positioning there with the 8.10 a.m. from Kingswear, which conveyed through coaches to London for the 8.35. The engine returned from Paddington the following day with a Weston-super-Mare express to Bristol, and the Wolverhampton to Penzance train onwards; No. 5011 is believed to have been photographed on the 8.10 a.m. Kingswear on this occasion. Newton 'Castles' and men also worked daily into Cornwall. One such turn started with the 10.10 a.m. Bath express as far as North Road, the down 'Limited' thence to Truro, and back with the 4.10 p.m. Penzance fast, and the 12.15 Sleeper from Millbay to Newton; No. 5011 was recorded with this duty on numerous occasions between 1928 and 1930, in which year she was transferred to Cardiff.

'Hall' class 4-6-0 No. 4903 *Astley Hall*, seen at the east end of Newton station, 1929. Her stay in the West Country was rather short, for just twelve months from January 1929 at Penzance shed. After similar periods at Banbury, Landore and Carmarthen, she settled down to a long stay at Oxford, lasting some 25 years. During her time at Penzance, she was recorded on the 8.00 a.m. local passenger from Penzance (normally comprising a four-coach 'M' set), returning with the through vehicles of the 5.30 a.m. Paddington (three brake vans from the Midlands and the North, and the four-coach 70ft corridor set from London).

This view was taken during the descent between Churston and Goodrington aboard the up 'Torbay Express', hauled by Old Oak-based No. 6007 *King William III*, c.1947. The ten-coach set (including a dining car) was the normal formation. The postwar train took 25 minutes longer than its prewar counterpart (which called at Churston, Paignton, Torquay and Exeter, then non-stop to Paddington in a total journey time of 4hrs 10min), although it made the same stops; all the extra time was allocated to the sector from Exeter to Paddington. The winter timetable of 1947 saw a drastic slowing of the 'Torbay', with extra (and lengthy) calls being made at Newton, Taunton and Reading, extending the journey time to 5hrs 10min.

CHURSTON

Late afternoon at Churston, with 'Castle' class 4-6-0 No. 4077 *Chepstow Castle* approaching the station with a local service from Newton. By this time, the trains through to Kingswear were largely worked by 4-6-0s, and 2-6-2 tanks were more frequently seen on Paignton services; twenty years previously, the line was home to many '45XX' tanks, with tender engines mostly restricted to the better trains, though at holiday periods the larger engines were much in evidence. No. 4077 was transferred from South Wales to the Newton division in 1933, and spent periods at Exeter, Newton, Laira and Penzance, remaining within the district until the late 1950s.

The Brixham branch train shunting fish vans from the refuge siding at Churston, c.1947. Brixham shed closed in 1929, and thereafter the auto engine was provided daily by Newton; during the 'thirties, '517' and 'Metro' types were used, being joined in 1936 by new locomotives of the '48XX' class. In that year, Newton's last two '517s' went, but the 'Metros' remained until the latter years of the war. Newton Abbot housed Nos. 1427, 1439, 1466 and 1470 during 1947, of which No. 1439 seems likely to have spent most time on the branch during that year. Churston goods yard (right) had an air of dereliction, though at one time, a goods shed was located on the right-hand road.

KINGSWEAR

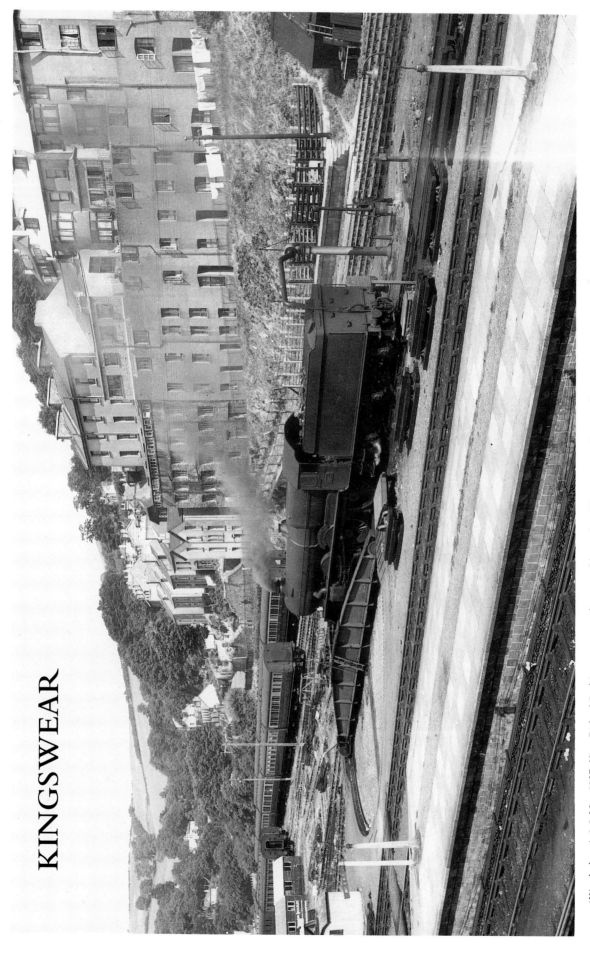

'King' class 4-6-0 No. 6027 *King Richard I* taking water on the turntable road at Kingswear, early one afternoon, c.1947. The class had regularly been in use for the 'Torbay' since 1928, with Old Oak and Newton engines each working in one direction every weekday. There were up to five sidings available for the storage of coaches. In the winter months of the late 'thirties, there were at least two rakes stored overnight, plus a number of individual or small sets of through vehicles for departure on morning trains.

Kingswear wharf, c.1930, looking north. At one time, a small 'L'-shaped jetty stood out into the River Dart, just beyond the steps in the foreground, with access for wagons via a couple of small turntables. The 45XX shunting in the foreground had brought in the pick-up goods which can be seen on the loop line in the distance.

STAVERTON

Staverton, Easter 1928, looking northwards. This small station was situated 3¼ miles from Totnes, close to the banks of the River Dart in a delightful rural setting. Despite its modest size, Staverton was equipped with a station building (left), goods shed and warehouse, and a signal box (right). The road from the village to Huxham's Cross ran over the railway by means of a consecutive pair of level crossings, one over the goods siding, and one across the running line (which can be seen to the right of the signal box). Around the time of the photograph, Staverton was manned by a station master, a porter signalman, a signalman, and a gatewoman at Staverton Crossing, some half-mile up the line towards Totnes. In the latter 'twenties, this was downgraded to a pair of signalmen and the gatewoman, coming under the control of the station master at Buckfastleigh.

Auto-trailer No. 32 on a Totnes-bound service, propelled by an unidentified '517' class engine at Staverton, Easter 1928. No. 32 was one of a pair allocated to the branch at this time, having replaced the 4-wheel stock a year or so earlier; the second car was mostly used on market days. During the late 1920s, Staverton was served by seven or eight trains in each direction daily, plus two further Saturdays only services. A goods train ran through daily from Newton Abbot to Ashburton and back, calling at Staverton for about fifteen minutes on both down and up journeys. The '517' class engines would probably have been introduced onto the branch shortly after the 'narrowing' of 1892, and Nos. 531 and 1472 were recorded there in autumn of 1896. They dominated passenger work on the line until the arrival of the interim 'Metros' and the new '48XX' engines in 1935/36, after which time they disappeared.

KINGSBRIDGE

The Kingsbridge branch came late onto the railway scene, being opened in December 1893. By the end of the Great War, '45XXs' had appeared on the branch alongside the normal engines, the '44XXs', and had virtually displaced them by 1922. Here, '45XX' No. 4549 is seen at Kingsbridge with the inevitable 'B' set, c.1929. The 12½-mile journey to Brent took 34 minutes, with a minute's call at each of the three intermediate stations. Two engines were allocated to the shed, seen here on the extreme right, with the first working the bulk of the passenger turns, whilst the second ran the branch goods, and a couple of passenger trips, for which a second 'B' set was required. There were three sets of men, two for the passenger and one for the 'goods', together with an engine cleaner and a shed labourer. A carriage cleaner was also established for the coaching stock, and all were supervised by the station master.

FALMOUTH

'4575' 2-6-2T No. 5503 entering Falmouth station in August 1931, with a curious formation in tow. At this time, many of the services on the line were run by auto-fitted 'Metro' 2-4-0Ts and a pair of trailers, but a few were worked by conventional locomotives, mostly '45XXs'. One such train in 1929 was scheduled for 'Two Trailers, worked by Engine of Falmouth Goods', not dissimilar perhaps to the combination in the photograph. Until its closure in 1925, Falmouth engine shed housed two locomotives (including a 'Duke' for the morning through train to Plymouth), with two sets of enginemen, a cleaner and a labourer. The '45XXs' were not regularly at work on the branch until the early 'thirties.